The Best
LEADERSHIP
ADVICE
I Ever Got

75 Successful Leaders Share Their Secrets

Paul B. Thornton

The Best
LEADERSHIP
ADVICE
I Ever Got

75 Successful Leaders Share Their Secrets

Inquiries regarding permission for use of the material contained in this book should be addressed to:

CornerStone Leadership Institute
P.O. Box 764087
Dallas, TX 75376
888.789.LEAD

Printed in the United States of America
ISBN: 0-9772257-6-3

Credits

Design, art direction
and production

Melissa Monogue, Back Porch Creative
info@BackPorchCreative.com

FOREWORD

———•◆•———

Imagine if you were given the opportunity to spend a long, relaxed evening with some of the most creative and innovative leaders in the world today. Among them were leaders from every level of society and every kind of organization. Throughout that enjoyable fellowship you were able to glean advice that would normally take a lifetime to learn.

Your invitation has just arrived!

The Best Leadership Advice I Ever Got by Paul B. Thornton is one of the most helpful and educational books ever written on the topic of leadership counsel and wisdom. Seventy-five modern leaders will share with you their own nuggets of truth that forever molded and changed the way they lead. Don't miss the opportunity to take your leadership to the next level!

Greg Thomas, founder of weLEAD Inc. and Editor of *weLEAD Online Magazine*

"I knew someone had to take the first step and I made up my mind not to move."

– Rosa Parks

TABLE OF CONTENTS

————•◆•————

ACKNOWLEDGMENTS

The March 21, 2005 issue of *Fortune* magazine included an article titled "The Best Advice I Ever Got." It was a great article that offered wit and wisdom from top business leaders. It motivated me to produce this book. The comment by Klaus Kleinfeld in this book is an excerpt from the original *Fortune* article.

A special thanks to the 75 people who shared the "best advice" they received in helping them become effective leaders.

INTRODUCTION

As a high school and college athlete, I was always curious about what made some teams overachieve. I concluded that – in most cases – the best teams had the best coaches. Of course, talent was important, but if the talent was even close, the team with the best coach usually won.

It was at this stage in my life that I became interested in management and leadership.

While at Ohio University I took Dr. Paul Hersey's course, Managing Organizational Behavior. He played a major role in the development and evolution of the "Situational Leadership" model. It was my *best* college course. His passion and ability to teach further stimulated my interest in management and leadership. In addition, I have been fortunate to have had several outstanding mentors who educated me in the theories and application of leadership principles.

I have discovered that there are many definitions of leadership. Mine is pretty simple: Leadership is the process of helping individuals, teams, and organizations become more and achieve more than they ever thought possible. That's it … helping others achieve their "A" game.

I also discovered that it was easier to define leadership than to become a great leader.

Leaders don't look or act the same. Some are tall, others short. Some are passionate and intense; others are low-key and quiet. Some are brilliant; others have average IQ's. One thing they all have in common is they are willing stand up, speak up and take action for a better future.

What attributes does it take to lead? I believe great leaders have five important attributes:

- ♦ **Integrity** – a strong belief in a set of core values.

- ♦ **Courage** – having the guts and stamina to make tough decisions.

- ♦ **Focus** – understanding the priorities that lead to success.

- ♦ **Perseverance** – the ability to hang in there long enough to win.

- ♦ **Ability to Change** – the ability to adjust your plans, thoughts, and actions to achieve success.

Certainly there are other skills that great leaders possess. However, the five attributes listed above are the building blocks needed to lead.

Would you like to be a more effective leader?

Of course you would. That's why you have this book in your hand.

The Best Leadership Advice I Ever Got describes the "best advice" that successful people from all walks of life have found most helpful in becoming effective leaders.

My personal guarantee to you is that before completing this book you will discover at least five new ideas that will improve your leadership effectiveness.

Read, enjoy, learn and lead.

"This book contains some of the best coaching on leadership that you will ever receive."
– Marshall Goldsmith

CHAPTER ONE

Advice on ...
Integrity

When asked which leadership trait – in a list of sixteen – has the single greatest impact on an executive's effectiveness, 71 percent of the 2,300 executives surveyed listed integrity at the top.[1]

Think about it. How difficult it is to get 71 percent of senior executives to agree on ANYTHING – especially when there are 15 other choices?

The participants in that study know the same thing you and I know – if the leader has sacrificed integrity, nothing else really matters.

[1] *Joint study by Kor/Ferry International, New York, 1985*

♦ Does it matter how often you communicate
  with your people if they do not trust you?

♦ Does it matter how committed you are,
  what mission statement you've developed,
  how optimistic you are, how skilled you
  are at resolving conflicts, or how courageous
  you are – if your followers do not trust you?

None of these leadership traits really matter if
your integrity is questioned.

Leaders who have integrity possess one of the
most respected virtues in all of life. If you can be
trusted, whether alone or in a crowd…if you are
truly a person of your word and convictions, you
are fast becoming a unique and valued person.

Integrity is the cornerstone of leadership!

Dianne Collins
CEO and Creator of QuantumThink®
Author, *Do You QuantumThink*

The best advice I ever received on leadership happened in a tiny quantum moment I call "Coffee with Isaac." When I was transitioning from corporate management to my own work in corporate consulting, I had the "bright idea" to write short romance novels for extra money. Though writing had always flowed for me, I was experiencing enormous frustration in getting this novel going. In a moment of delirium, I called Nobel Laureate Isaac Bashevis Singer, seeking his advice. Shocked when he answered the phone himself, I nervously blurted out, *"Isaac, you don't know me but I have got to talk to you!!"* In his thick Polish accent he mused, *"A philosopher turned marketer turned writer – this I've got to meet."*

Meet we did over coffee in a 50's diner on a street in Miami Beach named after him. When I shared my dilemma, he leaned over the table, intense sky blue eyes twinkling and staring into mine and told me, *"In order to write junk, you've got to have a junky soul."* I gulped the coffee. The message penetrated deep. I could only do what is true to my soul. I

13

have lived that ever since and relay that message to all of our clients. Do what is true to your soul and you'll express your gifts and talents to the highest and derive the most pleasure from your work. Generate the same intent for your people. When you connect to who people are and create the opportunity for them to work on what suits them best, what they love to do, *what resonates with their soul* – it translates multi-dimensionally to improved bottom lines and fine times. The other lesson learned: a moment of friendly, non-rational chutzpah can change the world.

Evan S. Dobelle
President & CEO,
New England Board of Higher Education

When I was a young man serving as mayor of Pittsfield, Massachusetts, during a very difficult day my city solicitor told me I had an easy job. "Easy?" I said, reciting all the conflict of the moment. He then replied, "All you have to do is tell the truth and do the right thing. The first is sometimes hard and the other means you have to listen to a lot of people, but at the end of the day you know what the right thing to do is and you always know what is true."

Oren Harari, Ph.D.
Professor of Management, Graduate School of
Business, University of San Francisco

The best advice I ever got was from management guru Tom Peters back in the mid-1980's. When I was first starting out in the consulting and speaking business, I worked with The Tom Peters Group. One time he and I were on a flight together and he told me, "The most important thing I can do for a client is to show up." He was being literal, and witty, but it's true. If I'm hired to give a keynote speech for a thousand people, the most important thing I can do for the client is, literally, to show up. But I've always taken Tom's advice in a figurative sense too. Whatever project or event I agree to professionally, I have to "show up" – that is, be fully engaged. If I don't feel I can be fully engaged and fully committed, I don't take the job. Showing up is ultimately about being trustworthy, being honorable, and being truly professional.

Matthew T. Kirk, CPA
Vice President, Corporate Accounting & Finance,
FOLKSAMERICA Reinsurance Company

My father was persistent in emphasizing the need to be honest at all times. In his mind honesty is absolute; there is no compromising under any circumstances, not even a "little white lie." He lives by this motto and through the years has often been called a "saint" in jest by friends and family. I have done my best to follow his lead and it has served me well over the years. No one can question your integrity or motives when he or she knows you are being honest. This is a strong foundation to build from.

Dr. Marita Naude
Director, Masters of Leadership and
Management (MLM) Program, Graduate School
of Business, Curtin University of Technology,
Perth, Western Australia

I have learned that trust forms the basis for most other activities. As a leader you need to trust yourself at a personal as well as a professional level. When you trust yourself (and display it through self-confidence and self-management), you will be able to trust others and get others to trust you. You also have to display self-respect,

respect for others and the environment. I learned that trust and respect cannot be demanded or bought, but must be earned. Trust and respect take a long time to earn but can be lost in just a few seconds.

———◆———

David Cottrell
Founder of CornerStone Leadership Institute
and Author, *Monday Morning Leadership*

My best leadership advice came from my dad. He taught me to always ask myself when making any personal or leadership decision, "What is the right thing to do?" No matter how I wanted to ignore or bury what "right" was, the right thing – based on the values he instilled in me – always surfaced.

Even to this day, I still have to ask myself almost daily, "What is the right thing to do?" That question has helped me protect my most important leadership possession – my integrity.

———◆———

Brian Morehouse
Hope College Women's Basketball Coach
2006 Division 3 National Champions

The best advice I received on leadership is from Max DePree, who was an extremely successful businessman in the West Michigan area. His quote, which I look at every day, is "Leadership is a serious meddling in the lives of other people. Leaders should be able to stand alone, take the heat, bear the pain, tell the truth, and do what's right." It covers everything a leader needs to do on a day to day basis. And it closely meshes with our theme for our 2006 National Championship year, which was "DTRT." Do The Right Thing! Every day, every play, on and off the court!

James E. Loehr, Ed.D.
Chairman & CEO,
LGE Performance Systems, Inc.

My father said that the single most important aspect of leadership is character. He felt that everything else paled in comparison. Honesty, integrity, and respect for others represent the essential core of all leadership. He also demonstrated his beliefs about leadership in his daily interactions with others. He clearly was the personification of his beliefs about values-based leadership. His beliefs and character had a profound effect on my leadership style.

Dr. Andrew M. Scibelli
President Emeritus, Springfield Technical
Community College

The best advice I received came from my father by word and deed. His words and actions consistently demonstrated the following: "Always treat people with respect. Never compromise your integrity. And be open, honest, and candid at all times, but temper your candor with compassion and understanding."

Simple and sound advice that has served me well.

Michael R. Knapik
Massachusetts State Senator,
2nd Hampden & Hampshire District

In government and politics, observation, understanding, collegiality, and honesty are the hallmarks of effective leadership. Nurturing and trusting relationships are the most vital tools a legislator can have at his or her disposal – both with constituents and with colleagues. The key to maintaining these relationships is the bond that is forged by keeping your word. A friendly, informed, and unshakably honest demeanor is the best way to exhibit and exercise leadership capabilities.

———————◆●◆———————

Tom Heuerman
Consultant and Author

The best advice I ever got was from Charles Freeman, the best manager I ever worked for, who said, "Keep doing what you believe is right, no matter what the opposition."

———————◆●◆———————

Jim Stovall
President of Narrative Television Network

The best advice I ever received was from an early mentor, Lee Braxton. Mr. Braxton had a third-grade education and became a multi-millionaire during The Great Depression. Very late in his life, and very early in mine, we spent a lot of time together. He told me that the best way to be successful, either personally or professionally, was to "always do what you say you are going to do." He explained that this benefits you in two ways. First, you will become known as a person of integrity, and second, you will be very careful of all the commitments you make if you know

you are going to have to perform. This has
served me very well.

Margaret Winkiewicz
Customer Service Representative,
Lenox American Saw Manufacturing

I've found great advice in books. One of the best
pieces of advice I read is the following: "Never
go back on your word." Simple, but powerful.
I try to always follow through on my promises
and commitments. Some people try to influence
me to make exceptions or cut corners, but I
must be strong and not cave. You can't have a
soft heart and let people step all over you. I try
to stand tall and be confident in the choice I
make. That is what makes a good leader. I try
to use this advice every day of my life.

Joan Goldsmith
Founder, Cambridge College and Author,
Consultant, and Coach

As a leader and as someone who hopes to enable
others to find the leader within themselves, I
found the best advice for myself in the writings
of Eleanor Roosevelt, our great First Lady. She

observed: "One's philosophy is not best expressed in words; it is expressed in the choices one makes. In the long run, we shape our lives and we shape ourselves. The process never ends until we die. And the choices we make are ultimately our responsibility."

I evaluate my success as a leader by cautioning myself to avoid falling in love with my own words and instead to rigorously evaluate the results I've produced from my actions. I find that, as Mrs. Roosevelt has indicated, I create myself anew each time when my behaviors mirror my values and I realize my intentions through my actions.

William H. Swanson
Chairman and CEO, Raytheon Corporation

My father gave me some wonderful advice that I've found quite relevant over the course of my life. He said, "You were given a good name when you came into this world; return it the way you got it." For me, that advice goes well beyond my personal life to encompass my professional life as well. Today, I encourage all of our employees to "Treat the name of your company as if it were your own."

Good managers want to promote people who feel a sense of stewardship for the company, a sense of responsibility to always behave like an "owner" of the company, like a member of the family. After more than three decades with Raytheon, I care deeply about its reputation and its people. I want those who are serving in leadership positions throughout the company to feel the same way; I want everybody in the company to feel that way. I use my father's advice every day.

———◆•◆•◆———

Leaders have integrity!

They have a core set of values and beliefs that guide what they think, say, and do. When leaders walk their talk they gain trust and credibility. Without trust and credibility it's nearly impossible to influence people to pursue new possibilities.

How's your integrity?

♦ In what ways are you truly living your values and beliefs?

♦ In what areas could you be more fully aligned with your values and beliefs?

———————◆•◆•◆———————

"Integrity is never being ashamed of your reflection."
– David Cottrell

CHAPTER TWO

Advice on ...
Courage

What is courage?

The dictionary defines courage as having the willingness to face and deal with anything recognized as dangerous, difficult, or painful instead of withdrawing from it. A second aspect of courage is "the quality of being fearless or brave."

The relationship between courage and fear is an interesting one. For some, courage means not feeling fear at all. But is that realistic? "Courage," said Mark Twain, "is resistance to fear, mastery of fear – not absence of fear." As we walk forward along a path, fear is there, too. We keep walking.

Leaders have the courage – the guts, nerve, and heart – to speak up and do things differently. Kevin Sharer, CEO of AMGEN, says that leaders are attempting to do something new. And new can be scary. It takes courage and conviction to put your ass on the line to make it happen.

Bottom line – if you want to lead, a necessary attribute is courage. Without courage people sit on their hands and remain silent.

Liz Weber
Founder and CEO
Weber Business Services, LLC

The most important leadership lesson I ever learned, I learned from my dad at his funeral.

At Dad's funeral, a man approached me to convey his condolences (I'd assumed). He shook my hand, introduced himself, and said, "You know, I never liked your dad. But he was a good businessman. He was a courageous leader."

Those words hit home. This man and my father had shared a somewhat combative professional history. Yet, this man's need to convey his respect for my dad overrode his personal dislike of my dad. His comment changed my life and how I viewed my professional responsibilities. I no longer felt the need to please everyone or to have everyone like me. Being liked as a leader doesn't get the job done; being respected does.

Before that night, I had run myself ragged trying to please everyone. I had tried to keep them happy and had tried to make sure they were happy with me. No more. I finally realized my job as a leader was to lead to the best of my ability and forget the unwinnable battle of pleasing everyone. Not everyone would like me or my decisions no matter what I did. All I could do was gather the courage to do what I believed was right and potentially earn the respect of others. If I accomplished that, I'd be leadership material.

———◆———

Stephen M. Dent
Principal, Partnership Continuum Inc.

I can't really remember if the best advice I ever received came first from my mother or my father. I can't remember because they both constantly reinforced it. The best advice was to have the courage to be authentic to myself. Growing up in a world of intense media and peer pressure, they encouraged me to stick with my values, even when they weren't popular. Because of that advice, I have charted a course that was true to me, leading me down unknown but exciting paths, and always leaving me better off and happier. As I reflect back on my life, I wouldn't have it any other way.

Eileen McDargh, CSP, CPAE
President, McDargh Communications &
The Resiliency Group

My first piece of advice came from my Dad: "Put
your brain in action before putting your mouth in
gear." When I make mistakes, it is often that I
forget to follow that advice. Notice the use of
present tense. Just because we KNOW better
doesn't always mean that we put our best lessons
into action. This means that having the courage
to say, "I blew it," is a complementary skill.

The second piece of advice was a line I read in
some unremembered book: "They don't care how
much you know until they know how much you
care." Whenever I start with a group, I ALWAYS
try to live in their shoes and understand their
world first. That puts caring before them in a
real fashion.

———————◆———————

Jim Ligotti
VP, Maritime Solutions at Ingersoll-Rand

One critical piece of advice I received and have
used throughout my career came from the best
teacher I have ever had, my dad. He would
remind me that delaying or not making a decision
was in fact making the decision not to decide.

You never will have enough information, you never will have enough time, but you do need to take hold of the moment and gather your courage and make the best decision you can. In today's fast paced world with so many interactions between events and information overload, I find this advice even more powerful.

Chris Conti
Executive Assistant
Top-Flite/Callaway Golf

My father always said, "Have the courage of your convictions."

The Senior VP Marketing called me into his office along with several other staff members. He asked us to review and comment on several ads he had developed. My initial reaction was that they were terrible. However, the other staff members were saying things like, "Good layout," "Effective use of colors," and "Clear message." I thought to myself, "Am I missing something here?" But when it came to my turn I said, "I hope this is a joke. These ads are awful." The VP then proceeded to tear up the ads and said, "It was an experiment. I wanted to see who had the courage to give me candid feedback."

Spencer Tillman
CBS Sports Analyst and
Author, *Scoring in the Red Zone*

One of the best pieces of advice I ever received was from my colleague, Keith Jackson. The legendary broadcaster once told me to simply say what I see. As an analyst, my job is pretty simple. If you know what to look for and can string a couple of sentences together, you've got it made.

Of course, it's more involved than that, but Keith has a point. What makes this nugget so valuable is that it works not just in my role as an analyst but in my daily dealings with people and as a father, husband, and businessman. I've learned that if you have the courage to speak the truth in love, say what you see, you'll always come out on top in the end. The last part of that sentence is key. There often exists a lot of water in between action and outcomes. It's sort of like raising children. It takes courage to make those tough calls when the threat isn't obvious to all parties concerned.

A good parent has usually "been there and done that," so their challenge is to resist the cultural tug to be a partner rather than a parent and make the tough call. Perhaps for fear of not being accepted or loved themselves, many parents fold and end up being friends instead of parents. In the end, the child loses. Say what you see, in love and you will always be able to live with the results.

———————◆———————

Ellen Leader
Leadership and Team Development Consultant, Authenticity

The best advice I ever got was really very simple, yet powerful. That advice was "to have the courage to just be me – the true, authentic me." Earlier in my career, my focus was on pleasing others as well as being a role model by highlighting only the positive. I also sought to maintain harmony, which meant there were times I watered down my opinion to avoid creating conflict. This style only got me so far in my career.

And then several significant people came into my life – my business partner and my classmates and professors from graduate school. Their feedback was that they didn't want to see just the nice, people-pleasing me – they wanted all of me, whether nice or not. They wanted me to take a stand, whether my perspective was the popular opinion or not. And when I did that, they felt more empowered and freer to be their true selves. We all grew as a result. Since putting that advice into practice, I have seen a dramatic shift in my leadership effectiveness. Although a simple concept, it is not simple to put into practice and it will be something I always work on. Not only does it require commitment and courage, it takes slowing down, being in the moment, and asking myself – what do I think about this issue, what do I need right now, and what is an authentic response for me right now?

Greg Thomas
Founder, weLEAD Inc. and Editor, *weLEAD*
Online Magazine

The best advice I ever received was when I was a young sales manager just a few years out of college. The early 1980's was a time before email, fax machines, PC's and software. Since I managed a sales territory that included all of Northern Ohio, I had a hard-working secretary who performed all inside duties while I traveled the territory securing sales. One day my boss, who was the National Sales Manager, made some crude and unprofessional remarks to my secretary. When I found out about the comments I was livid. I immediately sat down and wrote the National

Sales Manager a blistering letter telling him his comments were unacceptable and unprofessional.

As soon as I dropped the letter in the mail box, I had second thoughts. I worked for a conservative corporation with a rigid hierarchy. I could have been terminated depending on how the National Sales Manager felt about it. I was "on pins and needles" for about a week until he called me. We discussed another topic at length and at the end of the conversation, almost in passing, he said, "Oh, about your letter…it was unwise to send a letter this harsh. When you are angry, ALWAYS remember to wait at least 24 hours before getting anything off your chest!" I then realized that the letter did disturb him, but he had waited 24 hours before calling me to discuss my comments. He was setting the right example.

Bottom line – have the courage to speak up. But drop your anger before giving people feedback.

Bruce A. Hamm
Principal Consultant, Compass Solutions

The best leadership advice I ever received doesn't sound like leadership advice at all, at first. A former manager once told me, "Nothing in an annual review should come as a surprise." At first, that sounds like merely advice about how to deal with employee performance in the review process. I have thought about that advice often and realized there is something deeper. Courage and open communication is the theme in that statement. I work very hard to be open with my staff, peers, and superiors, and encourage them to do the same. I would rather have the unvarnished truth about a situation or their opinion of my performance than to find out later there was something that surprised them or me by lack of knowledge.

Mitch McCrimmon
Business Psychologist, Self Renewal Group

I've never been a leader in the conventional sense, but then I have an unconventional view of what leadership is all about. I see it as consisting solely in challenging the status quo – providing new directions. I call it thought leadership, the upward promotion of new ideas by knowledge workers.

How did I become a thought leader? Personal experience has taught me to question the status quo. There is always a better way to get the job done. Leaders generate ideas. They find easier, better ways to achieve the desired goals. My parents gave me the confidence and courage to lead by competing in the arena of ideas. At age 12 my mother said that I could become anything I wanted to be. We were sitting on a rock overlooking a lake and I remember how fervently she said it. She believed in me and that gave me great confidence in my abilities. My father encouraged me to think for myself and gave me the freedom to make decisions on my own.

Chip Bell
President, The Chip Bell Group and
Author, *Magnetic Service*

I invited a fellow consultant to assist me with a group of senior executives of a long-term client. She had heard me repeatedly rave about the CEO of this large financial services company. Her flight was delayed and the meeting was already underway when she arrived, preventing me from introducing her to the group. After listening to the team of fifteen execs in a lengthy, spirited dialogue over a strategic challenge, she whispered to me, "Which one is the CEO?" It was the highest compliment she could have bestowed on a CEO fond of saying, "Never add any more leadership than is needed." Great leaders have the courage to busy themselves with the business of mission and course, not might and conceit.

Judy Yero
Educator and Author, *Teaching in Mind: How Teacher Thinking Shapes Education*

The best advice I received was about believing that my ideas were unique enough – valuable enough – to be worthy of consideration. During the 1980s, I often felt tremendous frustration because solutions to many of the problems that plagued education seemed so obvious. I couldn't understand why others didn't see the same thing. Of course, I said nothing ... after all, I was "only" a teacher. But several years later, a famous educational "expert" would publish the same idea and the educational world would fall at his feet.

This happened repeatedly. Then, I attended a unique gathering of forward-thinking people – "movers and shakers" from business, medicine, psychology, the arts, etc. I was both surprised and exhilarated because many of the people I spoke to seemed fascinated by what I assumed were "obvious" ideas! On the flight home, I sat next to a woman I'd met at the conference. When I explained my frustration, she said, "You have to remember that you've spent a great deal of time and energy thinking about the issue. In doing so, you've synthesized ideas from a variety of disciplines and contexts. So what is obvious to you may not be obvious to others."

I didn't realize it at the time, but the woman who spoke those words was June Singer, a highly respected Jungian analyst. Her words gave me the courage and confidence to begin doing workshops and, in a small way, putting my ideas "out there." Eventually, it led to my writing *Teaching in Mind* and my present work.

Jocelyn Rasmussen
Founder and CEO, More than Speaking,
More than Singing

The best advice I received about being an effective leader came from my father. He taught me that my life is a precious gift and my talents are a grace that is not mine alone; they come through me in order that I might serve others. In my father's leadership model, the first and most important action of each day is establishing conscious contact with the source of all creation, the mystery beyond understanding. A leader's decisions are informed by a walking awareness of this mystery and they are not to serve the self alone but rather the highest good of all concerned. I don't walk in my father's footsteps because he taught me to have the courage to walk my own path, inspired by my own relationship with the mystery. He taught me to serve life, and this is the greatest honor a leader has.

Kenny Moore
Director, Human Resources and Corporate
Ombudsman, KeySpan Corporation and
co-author of *The CEO and the Monk: One*
Company's Journey to Profit and Purpose

My best advice about leadership comes from my religious background as a monk and through personal experience. Today employee surveys across all industries reveal three disturbing trends:

♦ Trust is at an all-time low
♦ Employees don't believe senior management
♦ Workers are too stressed out to care

When I was a monk, we referred to this as a crisis of Faith, Hope and Charity. What causes this type of crisis? Leaders? We seem to keep waiting for our leaders to take action, solve problems, guarantee job success – as well as keep us motivated and engaged. That sounds a bit unrealistic to me. It also keeps us in the throes of passive dependency: waiting for someone else to fix the problems at hand. My fear is that when I die they'll inscribe on my tombstone: "He was waiting for senior management to get their act together." It may never happen. I've learned to stop waiting, take responsibility now to do something meaningful…and move forward. The best piece of business advice I ever heard

was from a small, elf-looking lady with limited
corporate experience: Mother Teresa. And she
spoke it well…and plainly: "Do not wait for
leaders. Do it alone, person to person."
Unfortunately, Donald Trump would have had
her fired.

Just go do it
2009

300,000
12 months

It takes courage to lead.

It takes courage to speak up and challenge the boss. It takes courage to take a stand for what's right. It takes courage to go in a different direction from everyone else.

How's your courage?

- ♦ In what situations do you exhibit courage?
- ♦ In what areas do you need to be more courageous?

"Courage is facing your fears.
Stupidity is fearing nothing."
– Dale Carnegie

Work goal

————◆————

CHAPTER THREE

Advice on …

Focus

————◆————

Leaders have focus. They are clear on their goals, plans, and priorities. To illustrate the power of focus, author and consultant Lee J. Colan compares the sun and a laser. He explains:

The sun is a powerful source of energy. It showers the earth with billions of kilowatts of energy every hour. Yet with minimal protection, say a hat and some sunscreen, you can bask in the sunlight for hours with few negative effects.

On the other hand, a laser uses a weak source of energy and focuses it in a cohesive stream of light, producing intense heat and power. With a laser, you can drill a hole in a diamond or defeat a cancer. That's the power of focus!

The truth is that it's usually leaders, not followers, who are responsible for frequent changes in priorities and team direction. Beware! If your focus is always changing, expect nothing but frustrated employees. If you stay focused, you increase the likelihood that your team will meet its goals.

Maintaining a laser-sharp focus isn't easy. Without question, you will face distractions that pull you away from your vision. That's okay as long as you quickly get back on track. Your job is to continually hone your focus, communicate the vision, and keep the team on target.

Ken Shelton
Founding Editor and Publisher,
Leadership Excellence

Here's the best advice I ever received about being an effective leader:

When I first starting working with Stephen R. Covey as the ghostwriter on *The 7 Habits of Highly Effective People* (1984), I was impressed with the simplicity and power of Habit 1: "Be proactive." What that habit advises me is this: You are not being paid for your time spent in going through the motions, only for your contribution. Highly effective leaders make a much greater contribution not by reacting to conditions and situations, but rather by pro-acting or taking initiative to envision a desired state and involving people in charting and executing a plan to get there. I learned that by being proactive, learning to be efficient in results and effective in relationships, I could achieve more of my priority "first things" and influence more people.

_ Weekley
David Weekley Homes
Fortune **Magazine's "Top 100 Companies to Work For" five years in a row.**

My business coach, Flip Flippen, provided me advice I remind myself every day: "When dealing with employees, the leader's focus must be, 'My goal is your success.'"

Rec to Rec
Success will come

Michael D. Niziolek
Vice President, Human Resources,
Hasbro Games

It came from my father. Although these may not have been his exact words, the essence was that "the only time the score ever counts is when the game is over." If you know your goal and are truly committed to and believe in it, then you cannot allow yourself to become discouraged by setbacks. If you focus on what needs to be done and ignore the negativity of those who are all too eager to see you fail, then your goals and dreams will become a reality.

Milton Rosenberg
President, Bernie's Appliance, TV, and Bedding

My father, Bernie, taught me to stay focused and committed to my values as I pursued my passions. Most memorable for me were my father's relationships with, and commitment to, his employees and customers.

* * *

Jay Christensen, CHE, CPA
CEO, Mahaska Health Partnership

My mother inspired leadership development in me by establishing performance standards at an early age, without actually specifying the standards. That may sound strange, but she did it by pushing me to set high standards. When I was a freshman in high school, I brought home a report card with straight A's. I was a good student, but certainly not a 4.0 always. As I proudly presented my report card to Mom, with my announcement that I had finally met her standards, she had a very different perspective than I expected. She said, "I didn't ever say you had to get straight A's. I just told you that I expected you to do your best." In that very statement, she provided me the chance to set the bar and be accountable for the results. It was my first memory of empowerment, and that drive has remained etched in my memory for over 30 years.

* * *

Thomas A. Goodrow
Founder and President, NACCE (National Association for Community College Entrepreneurship)

Focus, Focus, Focus! This by far is the best advice I have learned through personal experience. Do one thing better than everyone else, no matter what it is, and you'll enjoy leadership success. Fight off all temptations to be distracted and unfocused by entertaining opportunities that compete with your core entrepreneurial mission, otherwise you'll become vulnerable to your competition. Lastly, take time to listen to everyone, but always remember to follow no one except your peaceful balance of intuition and intellect.

* * *

Klaus Kleinfeld
CEO, Siemens

The best advice I ever got was from an old friend of the family and it goes like this: Whenever you take on a new position, before you jump in and get bogged down in the details, sit down, lean back, close your eyes, and think about what you really want to achieve and how you want things to look in a couple of years. And only then – once you have a clear vision in front of your inner eye – start executing so that things will move in that direction.

Mario Morino
Chairman, Venture Philanthropy Partners

The best advice came from my business partner, and his nuggets of wisdom were many. First, it's all about focus and execution...ideas are great, strategy is wonderful and necessary, but if you don't do the boring "blocking and tackling" day in and day out, you won't make it. Second, remember that the twin thieves of success are "ego" and "greed," for they ruin more businesses and wreck more lives than anything else. Deal with these as you see success, and you will really be successful!

Debbe Kennedy
President, CEO and Founder, Global Dialogue
Center and Leadership Solutions Companies,
and Author, *Action Dialogues* **and** *Breakthrough!*

His name was *Bookie*. I was a young manager at IBM just promoted to my first staff assignment in a regional marketing office. For reasons I can't explain, he called me into his office while I was visiting his location. "I want to pass along a little advice to you," he offered unsolicited. He shared his *secrets to success*: "Jobs, missions, titles and organizations will come and go. Business is dynamic. It changes. Don't focus your goals toward any of these. What you need to do is learn to master the skills that will allow you to work anywhere.

There are four skills: The ability to develop an idea, effectively plan for its implementation, execute second-to-none, and achieve superior results time after time. Seek jobs and opportunities with this in mind. Forget what others do. Work to be known for delivering excellence. It speaks for itself and it opens doors." Bookie's words remain fresh in my mind. They were instrumental in shaping my direction, future and achievements. He was right-on! I've always wished he knew.

Brigitte A. Kirk
Director – Financial Planning and Analysis,
Horizon Blue Cross Blue Shield of New Jersey

There is one thing I learned early in my career that has proven its worth many times over. It has to do with making things simple. No matter how daunting the task, focus requires that a leader be able to translate the complex into no more than three major points or action items that all stakeholders will understand. The application of this concept has been most helpful in achieving both organizational and personal goals that otherwise might not have been met.

───◆◆◆───

Sandra Schrift
Personal Success and Business Coach to
Professional Speakers

Catherine Mackey, Ph.D., senior vice president of Pfizer Global Research and Development, provided me with three concepts of leadership:

1. Create a compelling vision and get my clients to go there.
2. My core values – integrity, courage, credibility, and honesty – will gain people's trust.
3. To focus on my journey and lead people to the side of goodness.

───◆◆◆───

Dr. Paul Kirbas
Senior Pastor, Church of the Palms

As a Christian minister, it shouldn't surprise anyone that my best advice concerning leadership comes from the mentor of my faith, Jesus Christ. Whenever Jesus attempted to teach his disciples the important principles of leadership, he always focused on the same idea: If anyone wants to be a leader, that person must be a servant. Jesus expressed this in words and in his own actions. When he wanted to model the real role of leadership, he proceeded to wash the feet of his followers. Jesus pioneered a new concept of leadership: Servant Leadership.

At first, Servant Leadership may seem paradoxical to true leadership. But more and more, the experts of corporate America are discovering this same truth. In *Good to Great*, author Jim Collins identifies the common key ingredients that propelled certain companies to greatness ahead of their peers. One of the first and most major discoveries was that these companies had a common trait in their leaders. He called it "Level 5 Leadership." But when you examine it, you soon realize that it is the same kind of leadership that Jesus taught and modeled thousands of years ago. As Jesus said, if we want to be great leaders, we must learn to be great servants.

Vincent Maniaci
President, American International College

Dr. Jay McGowan, President, Bellarmine
University, told me that you may think you have
ten things to focus on, but you really only have
one or maybe two, and three at the most. The
big question – are you focused on the right
things? Leaders need to be clear on the "big
ideas" they are pursuing.

Leslie L. Kossoff
Author and International Executive Advisor

The best advice I ever got was from Dr. W.
Edwards Deming. In simple, uncompromising
terms, he made it clear that there is no reason –
nor excuse – for waste to exist within an
organization, no matter what the size or sector.
Whether time, materials, money – or worst of
all, the ideas, ability and creativity of employees
and managers at every level – waste simply need
not exist. But it must be systematically managed
out of the system.

While to many, then and now, that seemed an
impossible and almost romantic notion, Deming
backed it up not only with his own theory but
through innumerable examples of the

commitment – and toughness – required to make waste history. For my part, helping organizations find and remove waste from the enterprise is one of my greatest joys. After all, the outcome is that employees, managers, and executives are given the opportunity to succeed every workday in everything they do.

As Deming would say: Nothing could be better.

———————◆—◆—◆———————

Chris Bartley
Men's Varsity Basketball Coach,
Worcester Polytechnic Institute (WPI)

My best leadership advice was a quote from Colin Powell. I keep this quote on my desk in the office and read it a few times daily to keep me on track as a leader. "Great leaders are almost always great simplifiers who can cut through argument, debate, and doubt to offer a solution everybody can understand. The result is clarity of purpose, credibility of leadership, and integrity in organization." I try to keep it simple and have a clear and compelling vision for our program at WPI.

———————◆—◆—◆———————

Kevin Nolan
President & Chief Executive Officer,
Affinity Health Systems, Inc.

What the people of an organization want from
their leader are answers to the following: Where
are we going? How are we going to get there?
What is my role? The more clarity that can be
added to each of the three questions, the better
the result.

————————◆————————

① to top

② Rec

③ Inv people to meetings

Leaders have focus!

The business world is very dynamic with new demands and opportunities occurring on a daily basis. The amount of information we must process and try to understand is overwhelming. Many executives receive over 200 e-mails a day. Add to that voice mail, the internet, world and national news 24/7, and it's easy to understand how people can lose their focus.

How's your focus?

♦ In what areas do you have laser-like focus?

♦ In what areas do you need to sharpen your focus?

———— ◆◆◆ ————

"If you try to do too much, you will not achieve anything."
– Confucius

CHAPTER FOUR

Advice on ...
Perseverance

One of the greatest success stories in American business history is FedEx. When Fred Smith created FedEx, not many others believed his concept would work – it was a little too far "out of the box." Their question was, "Why would you deliver a package from San Francisco to Los Angeles through Memphis?"

His Yale professor gave him a C on the paper that he wrote explaining his idea. The investment community considered his concept illogical. Would you invest your money or career in such a radical concept?

Mark Twain once said, "The man with a new idea is a crank until the idea succeeds," and there were plenty of people calling Fred Smith a crank in the early '70s. But, Fred Smith understood his mission, invited some committed people to join him, persevered beyond the naysayers, and in April 1973 FedEx became a reality.

You can imagine the excitement on the first night of operation! Fourteen FedEx planes in fourteen cities made their first midnight trip to Memphis. The packages were sorted and then reloaded on planes that would take them to their destinations. The entire FedEx team was waiting to count the packages and celebrate their success.

One by one they unloaded the planes. When all the packages were counted, there were twelve packages on the fourteen planes. Two more planes than packages! That is not a good business model.

Can you imagine how discouraging the first night's results must have been?

Sure, everyone was disappointed, but Fred Smith understood the long-term mission and was committed to persevere to pay the price of success.

Tonight, FedEx will sort and deliver more than three million packages. Revenues were over $40 billion in 2005. More than 300,000 employees are on the payroll, thanks to those first committed employees and the perseverance and vision of Fred Smith.

———— ◆•◆• ————

Markku Kauppinen
President, Extended DISC North America, Inc.

It's a quote from Calvin Coolidge: "Nothing in the world can take the place of persistence. Talent will not; nothing is more common than unsuccessful men with talent. Genius will not; unrewarded genius is almost a proverb. Education will not; the world is full of educated derelicts. Persistence and determination alone are omnipotent."

———— ◆•◆• ————

Charlie "Tremendous" Jones
Author and Hall of Fame Speaker

Many years ago I was selected, along with several unit managers, for our managers' training program. I had the largest unit in the company and was excited knowing that when the training program was completed I would receive the first appointment. I threw myself into every assignment wholeheartedly to make sure they didn't forget me. The training included several weeks in the home office and field assignments training new agents and assisting agency managers. The company began making manager assignments and to my surprise I wasn't first. Not only was I not first, but finally they were all assigned and I was still traveling around the country and getting home every other weekend to see my wife and four children. I was becoming more discouraged and bewildered each day that no one gave me any hope and I began to think they had forgotten about me.

I decided my career was over where I was but I didn't feel I could honorably talk with other companies while still on the payroll of my present company. I wrote a letter to my marketing VP explaining how I loved the company and was grateful for the opportunity I had, but since it now appeared that I had no future there, I would like permission to talk with other companies as I finished my projects.

I received a call from the home office asking me to come in immediately for a meeting with the senior sales VP. At the meeting the VP assured me I wasn't forgotten, but if I would be patient a little longer I would be a very happy young man. He explained, "We aren't promising you anything," but he added they had something special that wasn't ready yet. I was embarrassed and humbled by his understanding my impatient, juvenile attitude and felt the world had been lifted off my shoulders now that my hopes and dreams were back on track. A few months later, I was sent back to my home agency, which was my dream come true. The best advice I got was when my boss told me to "write all the resignation letters you want but don't mail them."

Someone once told me that if you don't find success, do the things that others neglect and be patient; perseverance and success will find you. In my career I've learned that when you're about to give up, don't. Keep going the extra mile and you often find success just around the corner.

Love

Lee Hargrave
The Hargrave Consultancy

Looking back over my business and academic career, the best advice that I ever received came from my mother. She was an elementary school teacher and drummed effective study and work habits into me, the eldest of three boys, at an early age. In primary school when I first began to bring assignments home from school, she insisted that my homework had to be completed before I could go out to play with my friends. It was difficult to sit at the desk and complete my assignments when I could see my friends playing through the window. Moreover, shortcuts were not an option, for my mother checked my work for completeness and accuracy. Only when I received her loving approval was I free to join my friends.

I've often reflected that this habit of "work before play" formed the foundation of a successful work ethic that has benefited me through life. As an adult, "playing" may range from pursuing meaningful avocations to simply wasting time. Over the years, my range of interests has embraced skiing, tennis, golf, duplicate bridge, poker, singing, and foreign travel. I've also wasted as much time as most people and enjoyed doing so. But every time I play, you can be sure that all of my work responsibilities have been fulfilled.

Mary Taylor
Senior Marketing Coordinator, Top-Flite Golf

My boss, the VP of marketing, told me, "You can achieve success and be a leader if you are willing to: Believe in yourself; find the right person to mentor you; and persevere."

John Baldoni
Baldoni Consulting, LLC
Author and Leadership Communication
Consultant

Leadership is about making things happen.
Advice I have received comes from my father, a
physician. He taught me the value of persistence.
If you want to make something happen with your
life – in school, in your profession, or in your
community – do it. Perceived obstacles crumble
against persistent desire. At the same time, my
mother taught me compassion for others.
Therefore, persistence for your cause should not
be gained at the expense of others. Another bit
of leadership wisdom!

Ken May
President and CEO, FedEx Kinkos

I can't remember who told me this but I have
never forgotten the message: "The good news is
never as good as you think it is and the bad
news is never as bad as you think it is."

When I was a young manager I used to overreact
to both good and bad news. Now that I've been
leading people for over 25 years, I have finally
figured it out. I no longer jump up and down at

the first sign of good news and I don't beat myself up too much over bad news. To use a Statistical Process Control analogy, I have taken my control limits out somewhat. News is just news and nothing more. I celebrate hard when we win big and I hold myself accountable when we lose big, but I don't react to every piece of news.

Joel B. Dearing
Women's Volleyball Coach, Springfield College

My dad gave me great advice about how to be an effective leader as a coach. He said, "Look for opportunities to give kids a chance." He gave me this advice by telling me stories over and over again of his high school coaching experiences, and challenging situations in which he found himself. Common examples of these situations might be injuries to key players or preparing to face seemingly unstoppable athletes/teams. Over time, I realized that he had a lot to do with giving kids opportunities. His hard work teaching and developing *all* of his players made it possible not only to give every kid a chance, but to put them in special situations where they could succeed. He taught me how to have a vision for what every one of my players can be, persevere beyond the challenges set before us, and make it my goal daily to help them achieve, more perhaps than they can even imagine.

Wendy J. Hamilton
Former National President,
Mothers Against Drunk Driving

The best advice I ever received was born out of adversity. The day my sister, Rebecca, and her little boy, Timmy, were killed by a drunk driver in 1984, I called my minister. He said I could choose to be bitter or better. I decided to fuel my pain into purpose and those lifesaving words have guided me during my more than 20-year career with MADD from a local volunteer to national president. Along our personal and professional roads we will encounter potholes and roadblocks. Those situations don't define us; it's how we respond to them that makes us who we are as people and leaders. Choose to be positive and productive, and you can survive the toughest of times.

Dave Hixson
Men's Varsity Basketball Coach,
Amherst College

One of the best pieces of advice I have ever received and continue to use and pass on is this anonymous quote: "Preparation is the science of winning." I am a strong believer in the power of preparation. If one has truly prepared and something goes wrong (I use the expression that a thread comes unraveled from the main cord), the strength of the rest (the core) of what you've prepared for usually makes this something which can be handled without crisis and panic. Along with this are two expressions from Rick Pitino's book *Success is a Choice*, which I ask my teams every year: "Do you deserve to win?" and "Have you done the work?" This speaks to the importance of preparation toward achieving your final goal. If you haven't done the work (preparation) the answer to the first question is an easy "no!"

Andrew Fox
CEO, Track Entertainment

The best advice I've ever been given is from my mother. She told me to never, ever give up. Ultimately, if you're working harder than the next guy, you will prevail. It might take longer. It might come at the expense of short-term financial gain. And you might not be popular while you're doing it. But if you truly believe that what you're doing is right, it doesn't matter what anyone else says or does.

Love what you do. And if you own your own business, surround yourself with people who love what they do. At Track Entertainment, I feel that everyone here is an extension of my personality; they all work hard, and they all love what they do. That's what you need as an entrepreneur.

Just like in sports, life is a game of inches. That means you have to play the game like every second is the last second. Keeping with the sports analogy, I wasn't the fastest athlete, or the strongest. But I worked harder than anybody else, and eventually I was the captain of my soccer team.

If you're willing to have that kind of commitment, just like the phoenix you can rise from the ashes. I'm a dot-com survivor. After the fallout from the dot-com bust, I nearly lost everything. But I kept working hard. I never gave up on myself, and I never gave up on Clubplanet.com. And here we are today, the internet's leading nightlife resource.

Paul J. Kozub
Creator and founder of V-One Vodka

The best advice I ever received was not spoken, it was from watching and listening. My father started his own craft business from nothing and grew it into a multi-million dollar company. I don't think there was any secret to his success; it was pure sweat and determination. He worked 18-hour days and made a number of sacrifices. He had good values, honesty and hard work, he respected others, and he knew that eventually all this would be rewarded.

That was my foundation, and now that I have taken the leadership leap for myself I carry those values close to me. Yet I also have my own take and it is this...a leader must have equal parts tremendous confidence and tremendous fear of failure. It is these two things that make me the business man I am today.

Leaders have perseverance!

Pursuing your vision – pursuing a new agenda – is hard work. In every endeavor there are problems and setbacks. Leaders don't give up or cave in at the first sign of trouble. Rather, they stay upbeat and positive. They keep hope alive.

How's your perseverance?

♦ In what areas do you exhibit a high degree of perseverance?

♦ In what ways do you need to show more determination?

———◆———

*"I do not think there is any other quality
so essential to success of any kind
as the quality of perseverance.
It overcomes almost everything, even nature."*
– John D. Rockefeller

CHAPTER FIVE

Advice on ...
Change

When Heraclitus uttered the words, "The only constant is change," in 500 BC, do you suppose he was envisioning the warp-speed changes we face today?

Probably not! Nevertheless, leading people through change almost 2000 years ago undoubtedly came with its own unique set of challenges and difficulties.

Humans inherently resist change in varying degrees...and clearly, the message of that ancient historical figure is: Get beyond the ways of the past and present and start looking toward improvement in the future. Can we improve without changing something? Does improvement come from just wanting improvement?

Obviously not. Author Max Dupree might have said it best: "In the end, it is important to remember that we cannot become what we need to be by remaining what we are."[1] Change is as natural as breathing, yet many seem to prefer to take their last breath rather than embrace change that can allow things to improve.

Today the "R" words are a requirement.

♦ Re-imagine
♦ Reengineer
♦ Redesign
♦ Recreate
♦ Re-invent

Change involves leaving your comfort zone and requires you to learn new ways of working. Leaders have the ability to change their goals, strategies, and methods of operation to meet the new challenges and opportunities.

[1]*Max Dupree,* Leadership is an Art *(Doubleday, 1989)*

Mary Cheddie
Vice President, Human Resources
SHRM, Board of Directors

The best advice I ever received was from my
friend Kristi Hermeier in June, 1975. She said,
"Learn like you are going to live forever, but live
like you are going to die tomorrow." She passed
away in November, 1976 at age 21, just a little
over a year after telling me this. Now, almost 30
years later, I still live and follow this daily!

Michael J. Dreikorn
President, The IPL Group, LLC

It was during a time of personal challenge and
while employed at Pratt & Whitney (aircraft
engines). The advice came from a dear friend,
Charlie Ashing of General Electric Aircraft
Engines. At the time I was confronted with
ensuring the new leadership above me recognized
the value of the organization I represented. The
challenge included various voices around the
greater organization that had their own
perspectives of value.

Charlie's advice was, "It doesn't matter how
many fans you have, one naysayer is ten times

louder than any outspoken fan. Don't worry about stroking those already on your side – your performance will speak for itself. Go out and find the negative voices and silence them." I have followed Charlie's advice since then and it has served me well.

———————————◆———————————

Lee J. Colan
Author of *Sticking to It: The Art of Adherence*

The best leadership advice I ever received was about being resourceful. A very wise professor once explained to me, "The key to success is not knowing everything. The real key is being able to plug up your ignorance within 24 hours." Initially, I responded with a chuckle since this advice came from someone who spoke 14 languages fluently, was a black belt martial artist and a race car driver, in addition to being a college professor! However, once I let these words marinate in my mind, I appreciated how poignant and practical they were. They became the bedrock of my future leadership roles.

I honed my ability to quickly assess talent and information so that I could confidently address any leadership challenge. This advice was liberating in that I did not feel like I had to be the expert at everything…or anything for that matter! It inspired me to build a strong professional network of experts. It also spurred me to learn how to ask the right questions to help identify problems, and then harness the resources for the best solution. In today's hyper-speed, mega-wired world, the standard for "plugging up your ignorance within 24 hours" has been at least cut to 12 hours!

Jon Miller
College Student

The bible has given me a lot of great advice about leadership and change. The apostle Paul said, "Test everything, hold fast to that which is good." This has taught me not to be afraid of change, to step out of my comfort zone and take risks. But also be aware of what's right and wrong, and to discard the latter.

Mary Jean Thornton
Former Executive Vice President & CIO,
The Travelers

Be curious! Curiosity is a prerequisite to continuous improvement and even excellence. The person who gave me this advice urged me to study people, process, and structures; he inspired me to be *intellectually curious*. He often reminded me that making progress, in part, was based upon thinking. I applied this notion of *intellectual curiosity* by thinking about the organization's future, understanding the present, and knowing and challenging myself to creatively move the people and the organization closer to its vision.

———◆◆———

Richard J. Faubert
President and CEO, AmberWave Systems

My artist-wife, Jeannette, said, "Make them feel what you feel before you try to make them see what you see." That was great advice.

Early in my career I was a P&L manager at GenRad. My goal was to run a successful, profitable operation. One day my direct reports and I were informed a particular "problem product" was moving into my area of responsibility. Upon investigation, I discovered this product was fraught with problems – quality issues, performance issues, delivery issues, upset customers, etc. The more I learned about the product, the more agitated I became. At my next day's staff meeting my normal approach would be to immediately jump into "problem-solving mode." My wife said, "Before you dive into problem solving, find a way to make them feel what you're feeling." At my staff meeting I asked each direct report to comment on what he had found out about the product. As the staff members reported on the issues, they discovered they felt the same sense of urgency I felt. My staff members went into problem-solving mode without any need for me to push them.

Bottom line – leaders connect with people at many levels. My wife taught me to first get in touch with what motivates people before dictating my solutions to problems. Feelings make powerful connections and can be a strong motivator. Also, oftentimes you need to get through the feelings before you can have a productive discussion about the problem and possible solutions.

———————◆◆◆———————

Scott Simmerman, Ph.D.
Managing Partner,
Performance Management Company and
Author, *Square Wheels® Illustrations*

I was sitting with Roger Bourdon, an old friend, at a conference and sharing my thoughts on a presentation I had just made. One of the cartoons I used was of a wagon rolling downhill with the wagon puller – the leader – with his back to the wagon digging in his heels. Roger's reaction was to identify this situation as a commonality in most organizations. The quote he used has stayed with me for more than a dozen years and represents one of the key learning points I make about change and commitment: "Nobody ever washes a rental car." If you cannot create some ownership about what is happening, how can you expect people to support the effort? People will resist things done to them but support those things that they own.

Julianne Kuhlmann
Principal Leadership Coach, Kool Results

My story is not grand and comes from humble beginnings that now reflect powerful results, both personally and professionally.

My friend, my role model, my mentor, my boss gave me the best encouragement way back when I had little regard for myself and my ability. He said, "I believe in you!" He challenged me, he encouraged me, he guided me and he knew I could do it, way before I did! I went on to work with Australian indigenous groups and with isolated rural women in business. In the early 1990's I broke new ground by taking training programs out to them, including using a suite of laptops to run computing workshops. I broke down the barriers between the wider world and the small community.

Recognizing that there are better ways of doing things leads to improved outcomes in people's lives. My passion today as a leader is the belief I have in myself and the potential I see in those people who enter my life.

———◆·◆·◆———

Gail Kasper
Motivational Strategist, Keynote Speaker and
Professional Trainer

The best leadership advice that I ever received, I learned from children. During my reign as Mrs. New Jersey, I had the opportunity to visit one of the neighboring grade schools. I watched as the children played during recess. The girls were beauty queens, the boys were army soldiers. I thought back to a time as a child where I was a movie star and producer. Children have something powerful that grown-ups lack – the ability to be creative. 90% of 5-year-olds are creative; only 2% of 40-year-olds are creative.

Yet, the strongest leaders are those that explore their creative side and think outside of the box.

They treat a tried-and-tested theory as though it is the first time they have ever heard it. They hear their people and are open to their thoughts, ideas, and techniques.

Great leaders know that being number one is not an accident, and neither is staying number one. They realize that continuous improvement is an everyday occurrence and the growth of each individual as well as the team is a constant evolution.

———◆•◆•◆———

Col. Frank Budd
Director, Organizational Health Center,
Kirtland Air Force Base, New Mexico

One of my direct reports told me one day, "You say you have an open door policy, but many people are intimidated by you and end up saying things to someone else they should be saying to you." Well, that was a reality check on my worldview of my leadership. I ended up sitting down with all my junior staff and truly opened the door – emotionally speaking – and learned a lot about my non-verbals, and how folks interpreted my actions. I didn't even have to contract out for a 360 degree feedback. I learned my most invaluable lesson: Establish regular communication with your people; invite and receive all feedback; and focus on relationships first, then the metrics, processes, and goals.

Beverly Kaye
Founder/CEO, Career Systems International

My best advice came from a mentor and deeply respected colleague. Frederic Hudson is an author, lecturer, consultant, and founder of The Fielding Institute and The Hudson Institute. Frederic is considered the "father" of mid-life adult development. I think the advice he gave me is important not just for leaders in mid-life, but for any leader at any age and at any level.

When I turned 50 (many years ago!) I decided that I wanted a day with Frederic as my birthday present. I completed a 38-page questionnaire and then drove to Santa Barbara to think about the next decade of my life. Frederic said many things that day, but one that is forever etched in my mind are these words: "Beverly, don't base your 50's on who you were in your 40's. Turn around and march into your 50's based on the way you want it to be." A great message! I think that every effective leader needs to consider when it is time to change old ways.

Often we continue a course of action because it worked for us in the past and we don't look for new alternatives or (heaven forbid) an entirely new game plan. Leaders need to take time to stop and look at their past decisions and behaviors and create the new path when it is warranted, even if it means taking risks. The most effective leaders I know are not afraid of accepting that there might just be a better way.

--- ❖ ---

Alden Davis
Business Effectiveness Consultant,
Pratt & Whitney Division of
United Technologies Corporation

It was 1984 and just-in-time manufacturing held the keys to unlock the improvements needed in the old factory where I started my career. Leading this type of change was not easy because people were heavily invested in the past. It became slow, tedious, political and personal. I was amazed how people didn't "get it"; they did not have the same level of passion and commitment for the future. My energy shifted. I became argumentative, judgmental and frustrated. I would mutter.

Col. Jim Hickling stopped me one day and said, "Alden, you catch more flies with honey than vinegar." I thought the statement was trite and missed the seriousness of the situation. But I knew that Jim said it as a mentor and friend… because he said it with warmth, a smile, a caring attitude and at the right moment. Jim woke me up with that advice. He made me conscious of my behaviors. He pulled me back across the counter-productive line that I had crossed. I had lost sight of the mission and let it become personal. My honey had indeed become vinegar and Jim stepped in with the right words at the right time to keep me from crashing.

———◆◆◆———

Janice Deskus
Vice President, Human Resources,
AETNA

Very early in my career I was asked to pull together a five-year strategic plan. I worked very hard on the task and felt I had done a good job. When the report was complete I shared my findings with my supervisor, the head of Strategic Planning. As we reviewed the document, he found "opportunities for improvement" on every page and on every page I explained to him why I thought what I had done was on target.

Finally, after listening to my rebuttals page after page he told me, "There is nothing wrong with making mistakes, but there is something wrong with not learning from them." Those words have rung in my ears for over 15 years. Every time I feel myself getting defensive I reflect on his words, listen and learn.

——————•◆•——————

Denny Rydberg
President, Young Life

The best advice I ever got for leadership was from the Old Testament, Proverbs 29:18. "Where there is no vision, the people perish." I think that is true for leadership. If you don't present a compelling vision, there is no reason for anyone to follow. Vision comes first; action follows.

——————•◆•——————

John Nicoletta
Leadership Consultant

My first boss said, "Separate the 'what' from the 'how.' Distinguish between what has to be done and how difficult it will be to get it done. Break the tasks into bite size pieces. Take small steps. Gain momentum."

——————•◆•——————

Margaret Wheatley
Author

I was interviewing a woman who had spent 40 years creating a very successful community. I asked her how she did it and she replied, "Little by little, one step at a time." I consider this to be the wisest advice I ever received about how change happens. It has helped me start things without worrying about where they're going. I just know that we have to begin. I also know that we don't serve our cause if we spend too much time developing a comprehensive plan instead of getting started. Those plans are bound to change as we get into the work. We do have to have a strong focus, intention, and will. And good relationships. Then we begin, step by step, little by little.

What's interesting about this advice is that I didn't receive it until recently. What it did was illuminate what I had also discovered doing my work and living my life.

Danny O. Snow
Author/Publisher and Journalist

It may be a cliche, but I'd paraphrase the famous 12-step prayer: "God grant me the strength to change the things I can, the serenity to accept the things I can't, and the wisdom to know the difference." I'm not too much of a drinking man, but I feel that this advice applies to so many other areas in life that it deserves consideration.

Ira Rubenzahl
President,
Springfield Technical Community College

While I was a student at MIT, Kurt Gottfried, a professor of physics from Austria, said, "Americans should read more history. In Europe, history is a part of our education and we see the world more clearly." To lead an organization you have to not only understand current reality but also envision what could be. To understand the "what is" condition, it's important to know the history of the organization – the people, defining moments, successes and failures. Only then can you begin to understand how to take the organization to the next level.

The second piece of advice that stands out is from Phil Austin, president of the University of

Connecticut. He said, "The role of a college president is to be a cheerleader." Leaders help people and organizations change, grow, and become something better. Change can be scary. Leaders have to encourage people and support them even if a particular initiative fails. A cheerleader emphasizes the positive values of the organization that are anchors during times of change.

———◆•◆•◆———

Marshall Goldsmith
Founder, Marshall Goldsmith Partners, and
Founding Director, A4SL-The Alliance for
Strategic Leadership

Dr. Fred Case was my dissertation advisor, boss, and head of the LA City Planning Commission. He growled, "Marshall, what's wrong? I am getting feedback from City Hall that you are negative and judgmental."

"You can't believe the inefficiencies that I see!" I ranted.

"What a stunning breakthrough!" Dr. Case sarcastically replied. "You, Marshall Goldsmith, have discovered our city government is inefficient! Is anything else bothering you?"

I angrily shared minor examples of political favoritism. Dr. Case was now laughing. "Stunning breakthrough number two!" he chuckled. "Your profound investigative skills have led you to discover that politicians may favor benefactors more than opponents." Then he delivered the advice I will never forget. "Marshall," he explained, "you are becoming a 'pain in the butt.' You are not helping your clients, me or yourself. I am going to give you two options: A – Continue to be negative and judgmental. If you do this, you will be fired; you may never graduate and will have wasted the last four years of your life. B – Start having fun. Make a constructive difference, but do it in a way that is positive for you and the people you meet. My advice is simple. You are young. Life is short. Start having fun. What option are you going to choose, son?"

I laughed and replied, "Dr. Case, I think it is time for me to have some fun!" I learned a great lesson from Dr. Case. Real leaders are not people who can point out what is wrong. Real leaders are people who can make things better. Dr. Case didn't just help me become a better consultant. He helped me have a better life!

Leaders have the ability to change!

Leaders are excited and motivated to discover new ideas, new possibilities. The best leaders are not vested in the status quo. They view each day as another opportunity to discover the next step towards excellence.

How do you rate your ability to change?

- ♦ In what ways are you proficient at introducing and managing change?

- ♦ In what areas do you need to improve your ability to change?

"It is not the strongest of the species that survive,
nor the most intelligent,
but the one most responsive to change."
– Charles Darwin

CHAPTER SIX

---◆•◆---

What's Possible ...
My Advice for Leaders

---◆•◆---

What does it take to be an effective leader?

Step 1 – Build a solid foundation of integrity, courage, focus, perseverance, and the ability to change.

Step 2 – See, describe, and pursue what's possible.

The Possibilities

What's the difference between a cab driver and a leader? A cab driver simply takes you from point A to point B. A leader takes you to a place you hadn't envisioned or thought possible.

What drives a leader to pursue a better future? Leaders believe most people and organizations are underperforming and capable of achieving much more. They believe there are hidden talents, underutilized resources, and people eager to make a bigger impact in every organization. Leaders believe people will rise to the occasion if they understand the challenge and know what's in it for them.

These beliefs propel leaders to do three things:

♦ **See What's Possible** – Leaders search for and discover new ideas and new possibilities regarding people, processes, and performance levels. They develop a vision, a clear picture in their minds of what the organization can become.

♦ **Describe What's Possible** – Leaders describe their vision in a way that gets people excited and energized. They communicate their message in a clear, concise, and convincing manner.

♦ **Pursue What's Possible** – Leaders take
   action. They execute!

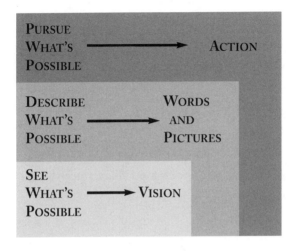

Seeing What's Possible

I have a vision! I have a dream! How do leaders
discover what is possible?

Leaders often start by focusing on what is –
current reality. New presidents and CEOs often
spend up to six months visiting company facilities
to meet with employees at all levels. They find
out what people think, how they behave and

what they accomplish. In his book, *Good to Great: Why Some Companies Make the Leap...and Others Don't*, author Jim Collins says that great leaders have the discipline to confront the most brutal facts about the current situation. They cut through the hype and spin to uncover the truth.

Current reality is one thing; what is possible in the future is something quite different. After lots of discussion, debate, thinking, and reflection, leaders begin to focus in on what is possible – what the organization can become. Author and consultant Marcus Buckingham says that leaders are compelled by the future. The future calls to them in a voice they can't drown out. It becomes the focus by which they engage their world.

Some of the specific actions leaders take to discover what's possible include:

♦ **Study the best.** Every chance you get, observe the best – the top tennis player, the most efficiently run zoo, the company that annually receives outstanding customer service awards, etc. There are always new ideas and lessons to be learned from studying the attitudes and actions of the best performers.

♦ **Change your mission**. Restate your business purpose or mission. A new mission statement can focus your thinking in new directions.

♦ **Be curious.** Ask questions. My favorite questions are "why" and "what if." "Why do we have that procedure?" "What if we outsource the HR function?" The right question forces people to truly evaluate how something is currently being done and how it might be done differently.

♦ **Start with a clean sheet of paper.** If you were starting out today, how would you set up and operate your department or business? What would you do differently?

♦ **Travel.** I'm a big believer in international travel. See first-hand how businesses operate in other countries. Experiencing a totally different culture always helps me see new possibilities and opportunities.

♦ **Leave your comfort zone.** Tom Russell, author, trainer and publisher, states, "When I think about what's possible I focus on what makes me uncomfortable. What lies just outside what I believe is possible? I find new opportunities and directions just beyond my comfort zone."

Bottom line – leaders discover new opportunities and possibilities in terms of both what can be accomplished and how it can be achieved. As a parent, husband, teacher, and coach, I have frequently asked the question – what possibilities do I see? What can my children become? How can my marriage evolve to a new level? What can my students achieve? If I can't see what's possible, I can't lead. I have no direction without a vision.

Describing What's Possible

What's the difference between *visualizing* a better future and *describing* it? Words – colorful, descriptive, and emotional words are needed to capture people's attention and imagination. Words that get people excited and energized to take action.

Everyday people are bombarded with hundreds of messages. How do leaders make their messages stand out? How do they cut through the clutter and get people to pay attention and fully consider their ideas? Leaders frame the discussion in a way that focuses people on the important principles, values, ideals, and opportunities needed to create a better future.

When developing your message, consider the following:

- ◆ Package your message with the right balance of realism and optimism. Be positive and optimistic but keep it real.

- ◆ Simplify the complex. Try to make sense out of situations that initially make no sense. Boil things down to two options such as "good-bad," "right-wrong," "present-future." Create a clear choice for people to follow.

♦ Use colorful words. Paint pictures. Former President Reagan once said, "A trillion bucks amounts to a stack of dough as high as the Empire State Building." If people can see what you are describing, they are more likely to stay tuned.

♦ Use emotional words. Words like justice, freedom, honor, respect, pride, and love can create a strong connection with people.

♦ Present the business case for change. Describe the most important reasons why change is needed. Most people want a clear explanation as to why they should pursue new goals and operate differently.

♦ Explain what's in it for them. Let people know the benefits they will receive when they achieve the vision.

Delivering the message
How do leaders deliver a powerful message?

They are:

- ♦ Passionate
- ♦ Energetic
- ♦ Animated

Where does the passion and energy come from? Leaders are excited about the possibilities they see. It's like a child who can't wait to get to the amusement park. He knows how much fun it will be to go on the rides, win prizes, and eat cotton candy. Leaders can't wait to get to the Promised Land.

What makes Martin Luther King, Jr.'s "I Have a Dream" speech stand out as one of the best of all time? His message was optimistic and simple – equal opportunity, fairness, and justice for all. He packaged his message with colorful language and emotional words. His delivery was animated, passionate, and forceful. His presence was clearly felt.

As a parent, husband, teacher, and coach, I try to describe my visions in the simplest way possible. I like using metaphors and visual aids to make my message come alive. Surprise, surprise, I'm not always successful. I've learned it takes time and effort to perfect what I say and how I say it. Soliciting feedback, editing, and fine-tuning my message are important steps in the process.

Pursuing What's Possible

What's the difference between success and failure? Execution! Leaders take action. They start the ball rolling in a new direction. They provide people with direction and support. Direction often takes the form of performance plans, which include the following:

- **Key milestones** – major steps needed to achieve the goal

- **Timeframes** – specific dates to start and complete each major activity

- **Metrics** – defines what will be measured and how often

♦ **Resources assigned** – people, equipment, financial etc.

Leaders don't get bogged down in all the details, but rather establish a roadmap to achieve the desired vision.

Pursuing what's possible means change. People must leave their comfort zone, which can be scary. You can help people leave what's comfortable in pursuit of a better future by doing the following:

♦ **Provide psychological support** – Encourage people. Build their confidence by affirming your belief in their abilities and reminding them of their previous successes.

♦ **Listen to people** – Take time to hear what people have to say. If you listen to them, there is a much better chance that they will listen to you.

♦ **Provide coaching** – Change requires new knowledge and skills. Help people learn the "how-to-do-it" part of the equation.

Coach, mentor, and train people as needed. In addition, help people apply their new knowledge and skills.

♦ **Provide cheerleading support** – Give frequent recognition and rewards for efforts and accomplishments. Plan and celebrate short-term wins. Momentum will increase if there are positive results early on.

♦ **Set the example** – Demonstrate that you are willing to change.

Leaders know that achieving their vision is hard work. Problems and setbacks occur. People get discouraged. Unexpected things happen. "Doom and gloom" people are quick to point out all the things that aren't proceeding according to plan.

However, leaders don't give up. They keep going because their vision pulls them forward and they know the result is worth the effort.

Leaders have vision!

Some people can't see beyond today. They have no vision. Other people see new possibilities but have trouble describing them in a clear, concise, and convincing way. Still others see what's possible, describe it, but never take the first steps to achieve their vision. To be an effective leader, all three actions – seeing, describing, and pursuing what's possible – are essential.

———◆◆———

"When you've exhausted all possibilities, remember this – you haven't."
– Robert H. Schuller

CHAPTER SEVEN

Summary

You can't build a skyscraper without a solid foundation. In a similar way, you can't lead without a solid foundation of integrity, courage, focus, perseverance and the ability to change.

Leaders help people become more...
- ♦ Confident
- ♦ Principled
- ♦ Knowledgeable
- ♦ Skilled
- ♦ Passionate
- ♦ Determined
- ♦ Integrated
- ♦ Balanced

How do they do it? Leaders see what's possible. They have big ideas and big goals. They have a vision of a better future. But it takes more than having a vision. You have to convince others that your vision is the way to go. Leaders communicate their vision in a clear, convincing fashion. Their delivery is passionate and inspiring. But leadership also requires you to take action, execute, and make it happen.

The big question – *How can you become a more effective leader?*

Great advice comes from many sources – parents, other relatives, consultants, bosses, co-workers, mentors, teachers, coaches, and friends. The important point to remember is to stay open, listen to everyone, but develop your own leadership style.

My Challenge to You

♦ After reading this book, write down the top three to five pieces of advice that made an impact on you. Read this advice once a day for the next ten days. Incorporate this "best advice" into your operating style.

♦ Identify the "best advice" you have received over the years. Pass along your good advice to those in need.

♦ Discover the possibilities. Probe, dig, question, reflect, meditate, and wonder every day. Look for and find the hidden talents in yourself and others.

♦ Describe what's possible. State your vision clearly, concisely, and convincingly. Use metaphors, paint pictures, and tell stories.

♦ Take action. Pursue what's possible. Set the example. Challenge others. Build confidence and teach, coach, and mentor as needed.

Perhaps the most important competency for leaders is to keep unfolding – becoming more and more authentic, principled, focused, clear, and influential. Even after achieving great success the top leaders are open to new ideas. They keep discovering and reinventing their leadership message and style.

Be the Leader,

Make the Difference!

About the Author

Paul B. Thornton is a speaker, author, consultant, and associate professor of business administration at Springfield Technical Community College in Springfield, Massachusetts. In addition, he is an associate professor at large for The Thierry Graduate School of Leadership located in Brussels, Belgium. Through seminars and individual coaching he helps executives, managers, and organizations reach their potential.

Paul has designed and conducted management/ leadership programs for many organizations. Since 1980 he has trained over 10,000 supervisors and managers to be more effective leaders.

In 1985 and 1996 he was the recipient of a United Technologies Award for Extraordinary Management Effectiveness. Paul is the author of numerous articles and seven books focused on management and leadership. His books are available at amazon.com and bn.com.

Paul can be contacted at PThornton@stcc.edu

Additional Leadership Resources

Monday Morning Leadership is David Cottrell's best-selling book. It offers unique encouragement and direction that will help you become a better manager, employee and person. $14.95

Listen Up, Leader! Ever wonder what employees think about their leaders? This book tells you the seven characteristics of leadership that people will follow. $9.95

Sticking to It: The Art of Adherence offers practical steps to help you consistently execute your plans. Read it and WIN! $9.95

The Leadership Secrets of Santa Claus helps your team accomplish "big things" by giving employees clear goals, solid accountabilities, feedback, coaching, and recognition in your "workshop." $14.95

Lessons in Loyalty takes you inside Southwest Airlines to discover what makes it so different ... and successful. $14.95

Monday Morning Communications provides workable strategies to solving serious communications challenges. $14.95

Leadership ... Biblically Speaking connects practical applications with scriptural guidance on how to address today's business and personal issues. $19.95

180 Ways to Walk the Recognition Talk is packed full with proven ideas and techniques that will help you provide recognition to your people more often and more effectively. $9.95

Leadership ER is a powerful story that shares valuable insights on how to achieve and maintain personal health, business health and the critical balance between the two. $14.95

The Next Level … Leading Beyond the Status Quo provides insight and direction on what it takes to lead your team to a higher and greater Next Level. $14.95

Monday Morning Leadership for Women is an inspirational story about a manager and her mentor. It provides insights and wisdom for dealing with leadership issues that are unique to women. $14.95

Leadership Courage identifies 11 acts of courage required for effective leadership and provides practical steps on how to become a courageous leader. $14.95

Birdies, Pars & Bogeys: Leadership Lessons from the Links is an excellent gift for the golfing executive. Zig Ziglar praises it as "concise, precise, insightful, inspirational, informative." $14.95

The CornerStone Perpetual Calendar, a compelling collection of quotes about leadership and life, is perfect for office desks, school and home countertops. $12.95

The CornerStone Leadership Collection of Cards is designed to make it easy for you to show appreciation for your team, clients and friends. The awesome photography and your personal message written inside will create a lasting impact. Pack of 30 (6 styles/5 each) $39.95
Posters also available.

To order, visit www.CornerStoneLeadership.com
or call 1.888.789.LEAD (5323).

711 005
Black
49,22
8,99

CornerStone▪
Leadership Institute

704 -002

★ Steve
228-669-1125
X end tues
XX 5:30